# POST  CARD

THE SEAL OF ARTISTIC / RA SERIES / BRITISH EXCELLENCE

*This space may be used for communication*

*The address only to be written here.*

Affix Stamp

PRINTED IN ENGLAND

*Wish You Were Here...*

# ISLE OF WIGHT

*from*

**Rol**

*for*

Bar

GW00702683

First Edition 1997

The Barracuda Collection from
Quotes Limited

Produced in England by
Key Composition, South Midlands Lithoplates,
Buckingham Colour Press, Hillman Printers
& WBC Book Manufacturers

© Robert Cook 1997

ISBN 0 86023 651 X

It's the first landfall for cross-Channel ferries and the Romans called it Vectis or Ictis – 'from the sea'. There are tales of a land bridge connecting the mainland. Once a river, the Solent is five miles wide, enough of a gap to make Wight something of a world apart.

Only twenty three miles east to west and thirteen north to south (at its furthest points), sixty miles of picturesque coastline contain 155 square miles. Within this is a rich diversity of wildlife and landscape, incredible in so small a space. The island is dominated by the chalk downs running from Bembridge in the east to impressive cliffs in the west.

The Solent is peculiar in having two high tides, so crucial to Southampton's mainland port and supporting the three island harbours of Newport, Cowes and Yarmouth. A nineteenth century railway boom created rapid links between London and the south coast ports. This, combined with Queen Victoria's enthusiasm for the island, which she first visited as a princess in 1831, made Wight a haven for Victorian visitors.

There was fierce competition between ferry companies. Tragedy resulted in 1899 when London and South Western Railway's steamer *Stella* was wrecked while racing a Great Western Railway vessel. More legitimate racing evolved as wealthy Victorians took to yachting. Cowes held its first regatta in 1814. The Yacht Club started a year later.

Originally the site of a Tudor fort, Cowes occupies both sides of the Medina estuary. Popular with King Edward VII and his Court, it has a reputation as home to the upper crust. Self-made millionaire grocer, Sir Thomas Lipton, son of a Glasgow papermill worker, sailed with the King. But the 16 stone monarch, affectionately known as

'Tum Tum', refused to lend a hand when Lipton's *Shamrock II* was dismasted in the Solent in 1901.

Lipton spent over half a million pounds on four *Shamrock* racing yachts, in a 32-year-bid to win the Americas Cup. For his fruitless efforts the Americans awarded him a presentation cup inscribed 'To the gamest loser in the world'.

Spending a lot of money for fun is the hallmark of Cowes. A Sunday newspaper recently observed how yachtsmen from all over the world set course for Cowes week at the start of August. And so too do beautiful girls out for a good time, diamonds and champagne. Cheekily the report suggested that size does matter, but only of a fellow's yacht. Hiding behind Riva sunglasses, the aspiring girl should dress the part, not forgetting the hired ballgown. She should head for the beer tent to learn who is who.

You don't have to be rich to enjoy the island's varied pastoral landscape and entertainments. There is a strong sense of community, though Gladys Bowe, who retired there in 1976, said she was called an 'overner' – a word from the locals' considerable and ancient dialect.

Holidaymakers, however, make their own temporary communities. Trinidadian visitor Vernon Church compared Wight with his homeland: 'It's very nice for a holiday, not only during Cowes week when all the toffs arrive in the their fancy yachts. One thing struck me was how large it seems after being told how small. One expected to stand at one end and see the other. My home island is 15 times bigger and we've got 14 times more people. Trinidad is a bit hotter but it has a similar feel, especially with good weather.'

Inevitably the island has changed since its Victorian heyday. Increasing popularity created a railway system, firstly from Ryde to Shanklin in the 1860s, developing to connect all major towns and villages. A plan to connect this network through a tunnel to the mainland came to nothing. The railways survived until motor cars reigned supreme in the late 1950s. Those without cars can use the 'buses provided by Southern Vectis, whose fleet retains a few vintage double-deckers for that extra bit of old world charm.

The 'bus company follows the island's Roman name but it was left to the Normans to spot Wight's military potential, building Carisbrooke Castle. Henry VIII extended fortifications, exploiting features of the natural landscape. That landscape and underlying strata support a wide variety of flora and fauna. An ancient hunting forest survives where red squirrels prosper and the National Trust lends a protective hand. Here is an island where 100,000 have the good fortune to live and many more are happy to visit.

Wish you were here!

The author is grateful for all help received during the compilation of this collection. Particular thanks are due to Initial Photographics for supplying images of the island's long lost railway system, so symbolic of what was first and foremost a Victorian holiday resort. Finally, thanks to Colin Stacey, Acadia PR & Design, Lois Bown, and Judy Ounsworth for their invaluable support for this endeavour.

Key to photographers:

| | |
|---|---|
| MA | Muriel Adkins |
| MB | Martin Blane |
| GB | Gladys Bowe |
| LB | Lois Bown |
| BJB | B. J. Brooksbank |
| RJB | R. J. Buckley |
| CJC | C. J. Chesterman |
| VFC | V. F. Church |
| NJC | N. J. Cook |
| RD | Reg Davies |
| BKBG | B. K. B. Green |
| DK | David Kaye |
| JO | Judy Ounsworth |
| RF | Red Funnel Ferries |
| WCS | Winslow Combined School |

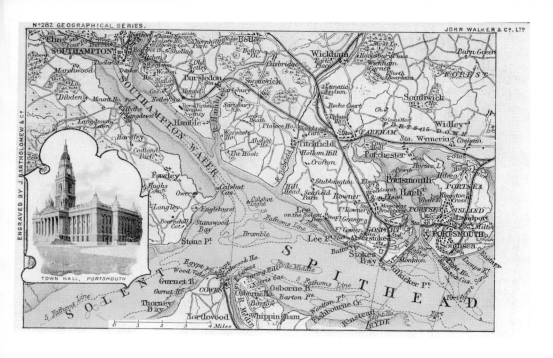

Early 20th century map showing passages from mainland to the Isle of Wight. The Solent benefits from double high tides. (JO)

This 1970s painting shows the starting guns for Cowes week, where glamour abounds.
(NJC)

For the rest of the world, who cares if your're building Bembridge Fort on the sands? 1956. (MA)

9

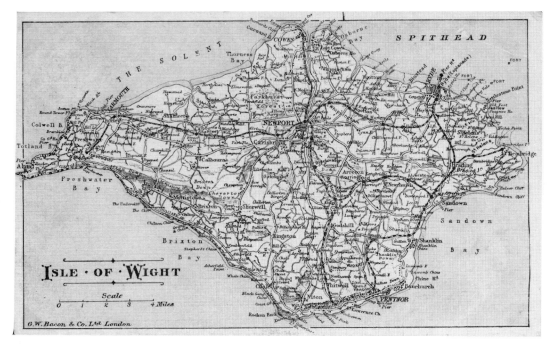

An Edwardian map shows the island, shaped almost like a diamond among the waves. (JO)

*Princess Elizabeth*, roll on roll off ferry, leaves Southampton c1938. Owners Red Funnel, celebrated 135 years in 1996 with a new flagship *Red Eagle*. (RF)

Passengers congregate for the ferry at Lymington Pier Station, June 1953. Foot passengers for the island doubled from 1937-48, to 441,000 and cars tenfold to 20,000. (BKBG)

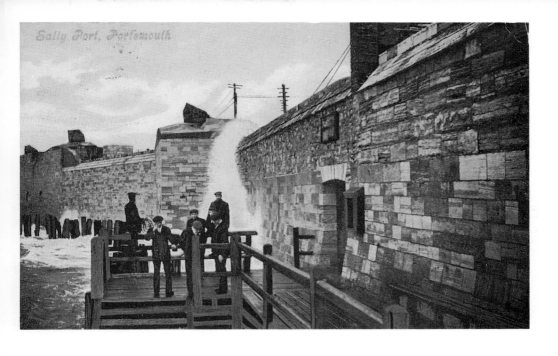

Portsmouth Sally Port, 1906: 'We are having glorious weather & a fine time. Lil and I are off to the Isle of Wight tomorrow'. (JO)

Beauty and the boat: a lady watches the *Osborne Castle* loading at Cowes c1956. (MA)

Southern Railways had a practice of naming engines after local place names. This is No 2 *Yarmouth*, an E1 type at Newport, 8 August 1947. (RJB)

15

Another E1, *Wroxall*, at Newport, August 1947. Wartime bombs fell on its namesake town, badly damaging the fine Palladian mansion Appuldercombe. (RJB)

*Totland*, a namesake loco at Newport in August 1938. It sounds like 'Toyland' and one wonders if the island's little railways inspired Rev Awdry's world of Thomas the Tank engine. (RJB)

17

The real Totland, 1904, shows what a haven the island was for poets like Tennyson and Keats, Totland meant *tootland* or look-out, a warning beacon on a headland. (CJC)

18

COWES. I.W. D.1005

Cowes c1930, when the Solent was crowded with steamers and swooping J-Class yachts under 12,000 square foot of sale, like giant butterflies in a rich man's playground. (CJC)

19

The Royal Marina, Cowes, early 1920s: 'Today we are having a tour round the island, the most beautiful place you can imagine. We are charmed by it, feeling better already'. (JO)

THE FRENCH FLEET SALUTING THE KING IN COWES ROADS.

The Anglo-French *entente* of 1904 ended years of Imperial rivalry between the two powers and here the French salute King Edward VII in Cowes Roads. (JO)

*His Majesty King Edward VII Yacht, Victoria & Albert.*

JWS 1058

Royal Yacht *Victoria & Albert*, Portsmouth 1908 when King Edward reviewed the fleet, on the Solent in 1935. (JO)

West Cowes, Isle of Wight.

Cowes, early 1900s, probably took its name from Henry VII's fortress, or 'cow'. Here 'There seems to be not trains stopped here. Two Germans were found at Freshwater yesterday'. (JO)

23

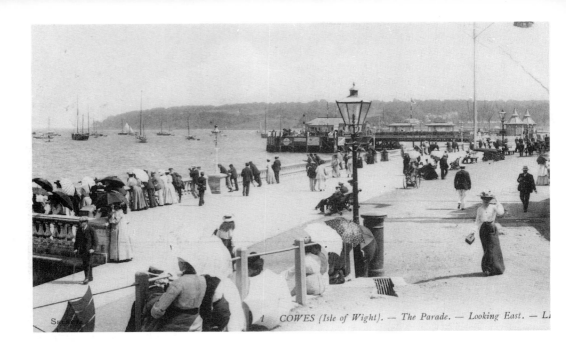

*COWES {Isle of Wight}. — The Parade. — Looking East. — L*

The Parade, Cowes, looking east. Running in front of the Royal Yacht Squadron, it extends west at the Prince's Esplanade. Prince Edward made Cowes fashionable in the 1890s. (JO)

PRINCESS BATTERY & LANDING STAGE, COWES, I.O.W.

Princess Battery & Landing Stage, 1904. The island was heavily defended during Palmerston's gun-boat diplomacy. A sixty metre tunnel leads to the Needles Old Battery. (JO)

25

The New Esplanade c1908 still offers a good view of races and regattas during Cowes week. (JO)

Departing Cowes station, 1 July 1953; the engine, an 02, is named after Fishbourne, which prospered as a car ferry-landing stage. (BKBG)

Class 02 local *Alverstone* pulls the 4.56 pm train out of Cowes for Sandown, 4 April 1953. (RJB)

Another 02, No 30 *Shordwell* waits on Ryde Pier in the last days of steam, 14 April 1962. The decision to close the railways was remarkable with 3m passengers a year in the 1950s! (BKBG)

Spencer Road, Ryde, J.O.W.

Spencer Road, Ryde, 1906. Ryde overlooks the Solent and provides a good beach and fishing. It has been popular for regattas. (JO)

Loco No 3 *Ryde* enters Newport with a mineral train, August 1947. Industry has included replica sports cars, and the Rookley Brick Company until the 1970s. (RJB)

Loco No 3 *Ryde* repainted in optimistic British Railways livery. Local poet Tennyson praised the Victorian railways 'down the ringing grooves of change'. (BKBG)

Newport shed was the place to spot the island's best locos. This is *Wroxall*, 7 July 1952.
(BKBG)

This powerful E1 loco is *Medina* at Newport, 4 April 1953, number one and named after the island's river, Medina, which almost bisects the land. (RJB)

Modesty reigns in this Victorian bathing scene at Freshwater. Poet Tennyson lived at nearby Farinford House and a local down commemorates him. (JO)

The thatched church of St Agnes was built near here in 1908. Tennyson lived at Freshwater for 30 years. In August 1969, Bob Dylan was inspired by him, to perform on the island. (JO)

Arch and Stag Rocks, Freshwater, I.W.

The detached arched rock, below the cliffs of Freshwater Bay, is neighboured by the stag rock, separated by erosion. (JO)

37

The Arched rock, Freshwater Bay c1920. This was severely eroded duringt he 1990s storms.
(JO)

No. 8 loco, *Freshwater*, an AIX type at Newport, 1 August 1938. All that's left is a two mile tourist stretch to Wootton, part of the former Ryde and Newport Railway, closed in 1966. (RJB)

Photographed at Newport shed, 5 April 1953, this chubby little engine, an 02, is called *Freshwater* too. (RJB)

4450. Sunset, The Needles, Alum Bay, I. W.

Alum Bay, just north of the Needles and famous for its sandstone cliffs of coloured stripes, is rich in iron salts and clay.

Newchurch Village, 1904, once centre of the largest parish, high over Yar Valley, included
Ryde and Ventnor, but changed little as the island developed. (JO)

Needles Lighthouse 1987, where hundred of ships pass daily. Usually the closest to an emergency is when a lamp or foghorn fails. Now unmanned, it is run by computer. (GB)

7403. COLWELL BAY, I.W., & THE NEEDLES FROM CLIFF END.

Colwell Bay and The Needles c1930. The 1863 Needles Old Battery provides a commanding view from 77 metres above sea level. (JO)

LUCCOMBE - ISLE OF WIGHT. 548.

Luccombe, two miles east of Ventnor, an untamed beauty spot, with a steep descent to the Chine; the landslip stretches along the coast to Dunnose Point. (JO)

*1  OSBORNE HOUSE (Isle of Wight). — North Front*
*Where Queen Victoria died January 22nd 1901. The King's gift to the Nation. — LL*

Osborne House, built to Prince Albert's Italianiate designs, within large gardens, with rare trees and a Swiss chalet for the children. Her favourite home, Victoria died here in 1901. (JO)

Council Chamber, Osborne House, I.W.

When Victoria died, Henry James wrote: 'We are to have no more little mysterious Victoria but instead fat dreadful Edward'. Edward gave Osborne House to the nation in 1902.

The fine Italianiate detail inside the Durbar Room, with Royal treasure roped off for public inspection. (JO)

*16   OSBORNE-HOUSE (Isle of Wight) — The Billiard Room. — LL.*

The Billiard Room, Osborne House. The State and private apartments are almost exactly as Queen Victoria left them. (JO)

49

13   OSBORNE HOUSE (Isle of Wight)  — The Dining Room. — LL.

Queen Victoria's son and successor, Edward or 'Tum Tum', enjoyed many a 12 course meal in this dining room.

Drawing Room,
Osborne House

Queen Victoria never recovered from Albert's death. When they lived here at Osborne
House, they worked side by side at their desks. (JO)

51

OSBORNE-HOUSE (Isle of Wight). — *Indian Girl.* — LL.

21

Prime Minister Disraeli had Parliament make Victoria Empress of India in 1876. This Indian Girl statue served as a reminder of her imperial glory. (JO)

Interior of the Whippingham Church I. of W.

Whippingham Church, built for Prince Albert in 1860 and attended regularly by Queen Victoria, where 'two of us have an afternoon off so we's out like two schoolgirls'. (JO)

53

ISLE OF WIGHT. CARISBROOKE CASTLE.

Carisbrooke Castle 1904, a Norman structure adapted from a Saxon fort sited on a 150ft hill. Charles 1 was imprisoned here 1647-48 before execution. There is still a prison at Parkhurst.

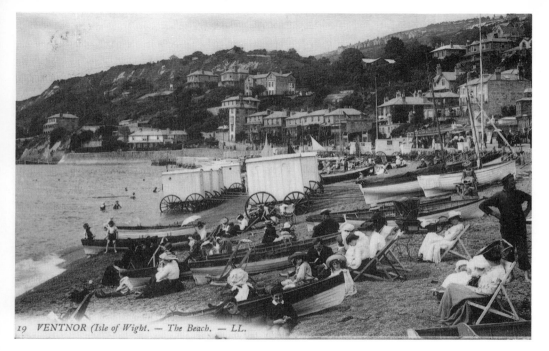

*19 VENTNOR (Isle of Wight. — The Beach. — LL.*

Ventnor, in the south east, grew quickly with the Victorian tourist trade – the Edwardians brought their bathing machines. (JO)

20  *VENTNOR (Isle of Wight). — Cascade. — LL.*

Ventnor and the Cascade where 'I've been packed off for my holiday' in 1907. The Empress of India and Empress Eugenie of France also stayed – 1874 and 1877. (JO)

Ventnor, from West Cliff, looks like an amphitheatre, below the 787 foot St Boniface Down, the highest point on the island. (JO)

The Cascade at Ventnor, a place of sub-tropical climate, here c1904. (CJC)

STEEPHILL
COVE,
VENTNOR,
I.W.

Steephill Cove, Ventnor, c1899. Sir James Clarke promoted Ventnor through his treatise 'The Influence of the Climate in the Prevention and Cure of Organic Diseases'. (CJC)

STEEPHILL COVE, VENTNOR, I.W.

17/6/05

'Where did you disappear to?' asked Ellie in 1905 at Steephill Cove. Ventnor changed from a cluster of fishermen's cottages, mill and inn, to a thriving town and watering hole. (CJC)

VIEW FROM EAST CLIFF, VENTNOR - ISLE OF WIGHT. 552.

Ventnor, looking from East Cliff c1904. The town has expanded within a complex of landslides, posing a permanent problem for property owners. (JO)

*8   VENTNOR (Isle of Wight). — The Downs. — LL.*

The picturesque undercliff, St Boniface Down. Sir James Clarke cited the undercliff as good for pulmonary disorders. (CJC)

Here locomotive *Ventnor* No 16 pulls a train into Ryde, 7 July 1952. (BKBG)

Ventnor Station on 1 July 1953, with local *Ningwood* letting off steam in those days of the 'old pull and push'. (BKBG)

IN THE LANDSLIP – ISLE OF WIGHT. 550.

The Landslip, northeast of Bonchurch 1909. Land between cliffs and sea, made up of blue lias clay, is unstable and has created attractive undulating hills and valleys. (JO)

STONE SEAT THE LANDSLIP - ISLE OF WIGHT 236

Stone Seat, the Landslip c1909. 'Two of us walked (from Shanklin) to Ventnor, the boat was crowded ... taken cold as I usually do on water trips.' (JO)

Bonchurch Pond shelters under St Boniface Down, not far from Luccombe Chine here in 1909. (JO)

THE OLD CHURCH, BONCHURCH – ISLE OF WIGHT. 551.

Christianity probably arrived about the end of the seventh century. Saxons built churches, then Normans. Swinburne was buried here in 1909 at St Boniface, Bonchurch. (JO)

Shanklin I.W. Old Village.

Keats stayed here in Shanklin; perhaps William Henry Davies did too, taking time to ponder 'What is this life if, full of care, We have no time to stand and stare.' Picture c1902. (JO)

Shanklin, I. W. Beach and Pier.

Shanklin took advantage of cliffs to the south east and has prospered due to excellent beaches. 'Walked with a Welsh woman who thought herself back in her own country'. (JO)

Shanklin I. of W.                    The Chine Inn.

1224

The Chine Inn, 1906. Where 'we had tea … we are all at it, early and late … and being so hot makes it worse!' The Crab Inn nearby carried lines by Longfellow. (JO)

71

THE BEACH SHANKLIN.

S 7918

Shanklin Beach 1910, offered all an Edwardian holidaymaker could want from deck chairs to fishing boats. (JO)

CLIFF WALK, SHANKLIN - ISLE OF WIGHT. 534

Families strolled along the picturesque coastal path to Luccombe Chine and Bonchurch c1908. (JO)

73

STONE BRIDGE IN CHINE, SHANKLIN, ISLE OF WIGHT. 525.

Chines are small natural ravines and this view at Shanklin is particularly pretty. The need to attract more visitors poses a threat. Blackgang Chine has a sizeable theme park. (JO)

74

Shanklin Chine c1899. Trees meet high above the slimy rock walls, and a 45 foot waterfall descends to a stream running past a fisherman's cottage, now a pub and restaurant. (JO)

75

In 1903 Emily explained 'I mean to take care of myself' but 'how cold it is' at Shanklin Chine. (JO)

SHANKLIN CHINE. I. W.

S.T. 186

The observation point above Shanklin Chine waterfall, c1909. Hilda noted: 'Threepence per person to go through this Chine but it's worth every penny.' (JO)

The Chine is 180 foot wide and nearly 300 feet deep ... with Chine Lodge, here c1932. (MA)

RUSTIC BRIDGE IN THE CHINE, SHANKLIN – ISLE OF WIGHT. 542.

Deep in Shanklin Chine in 1909, walkers going north east to Luccombe Chine could descend 300 rough steps to an unspoiled beach. (JO)

Chine Hollow, Shanklin. Isle of Wight. 587.

Chine Hollow, Shanklin has a wartime relic, part of the undersea pipe-line used to pump fuel for the Normandy landings, and a memorial to Royal Marines 40 Commando. (JO)

The Chine Road, Shanklin. Isle of Wight. 566.

A view of unspoilt beauty, Chine Road, Shanklin 1909. Shanklin is now a holiday attraction with outstanding coastal views, funfair and entertainment. (JO)

Shanklin. I. W. Luccomb Rocks.

Luccombe Rocks 1908 where 'These are the rocks Miss H and I climbed over with much difficulty. I have a cold now. It was so hot on land and cold in the water'. (JO)

82

Shanklin. Isle of Wight. 607.

A parting shot of Shanklin as it was in 1908. The restored twelth century church, St Blasins, makes a fine landmark atop the cliffs. (JO)

Engine number 22 *Brading* with a 'push and pull' service at Shanklin, 27 August 1966. These were the last days of the first line to open, a century before in the early 1860s. (RJB)

Engine number 31 *Chale* at Brading on the Shanklin-Ryde Pier train, 27 August 1966, named after a place where the bay was once called 'Bay of Death' and haunted by wreckers. (RJB)

Engine number 22, an 02, *Shanklin* at Brading – known for its restored old town hall, stocks and whipping post. (RJB)

Engine number *22 Brading* being prepared at Shanklin for the 10.14 am to Ryde Pier. (RJB)

July 1953, a long train is pulled by engine number 19 *Osborne* into Brading, the village once known as 'King's Town'. Brading had a working harbour until 1880. (BKBG)

Loco number 21 *Sandown* with the Brading-Ventnor service, 7 April 1953. The station name board gives a clue to the once comprehensive rail network. (RJB)

'Buses were an option for visitors, but this Southern Vectis Dennis Lancet and AEC Reliance were taken over for troop transports in World War II. (RD)

'See Sandown by Southern Vectis' 1940 Bristol open-decker – off from the Zoo on route 44 to Shanklin. (DK)

The island has become commercialised and Sandown experienced its earliest effects. Built at
sea level, this charming view c1910 shows the twin paddle steamer heading for the pier. JO)

SANDOWN BAY—ISLE OF WIGHT. 532.

Sandown Beach c1910: Gladys Eacher sailed on Red Funnel's twin-paddle *Lorna Doone* in the 1930s: 'It was very relaxing watching the paddles going round'. (CJC)

This is the Freshwater-Shanklin service hauled by number 27 *Merestone*, 7 April 1953. (RJB)

Engine number 23 *Totland* steams into Sandown with the Ryde-Ventnor service, looking smart on 7 April 1953. (RJB)

*Totland* near Bembridge, July 1953. Muriel King remembered in July 1934 'We had a hair raising train journey ... arrived late. It was a relief to get on the little train for Ryde'. (BKBG)

Isle of Wight's environment interests student of all ages. Winslow Combined School pupils study Bembridge Estuary and coastal defences in a session led by Mr Hampshire. (WCS)

View from Shanklin Cliff top c1934, by young Muriel King, who remembers the thrill of being there with her box camera, and was careful to count to six before closing the shutter.

Gleaming No 14 *Fishbourne*, an 02 at Bembridge, 7 April 1953. These engines were designed by Adams for the LSWR, introduced in 1889 and transferred to the Isle in 1925. (RJB)

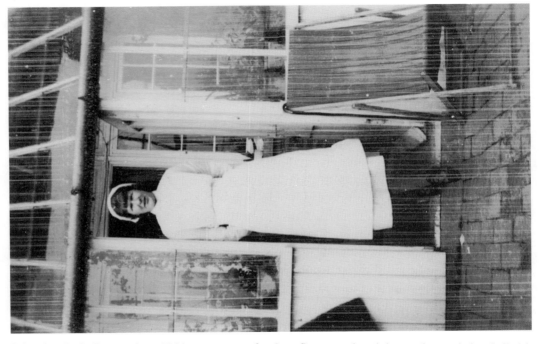

Islander Lois Bown, late 1930s, prepares for her first nursing job on the mainland. Babies usually arrived at night and she travelled to confinements by bike or Shank's pony. (LB)

Muriel Adkins remembers the long walk over Boniface Down to photograph this rocky beach scene near Luccombe in the early 1930s. (MA)

Shanklin Church Yard c1934: Alice Storey, Nellie King, Ted and Ernestine Storey. 'A Happy evening walk. Everyone was smiling. Mother had a nice straw hat with flowers round it.' (MA)

Muriel King enjoyed her holiday in 1934, (left) on the footpath over Boniface Down, and
(right) in Alice Storey's back garden at The Glorie, Shanklin. (MA)

Like so many before and since, Nellie King takes the air on top of the cliff at Keats Green, surrounded by hydrangeas. (MA)

An old fashioned paddle for (left to right) Ernestine, Ted (Storey), Nellie King and Alice Storey, Shanklin c1934. (MA)

Godshill c1905 where Lil wrote 'How do you like going back, I don't want to.' Not surprisingly! (JO)

Godshill c1932 and the motor car has arrived. Nowadays this place is popular with coach trippers for cream teas, souvenirs and the toy museum. (MA)

Godshill must have its railway namesake and here it is, No 25, an 02 at Newport shed.
(BKBG)

Two Shanklin beauty spots c1932: (left) the restored twelth century church and (right) on the cliff tops.

In 1934 on Bembridge Down 'We trod the rolling down, back to Shanklin town, mum, friends and me, past the leafy tree' – not quite Tennyson, but the island is an inspiration to all. (MA)

It's a rocky beach, where marine life flourishes, near Shanklin c1934. (MA)

The normal holiday pictures that escape 'normal' books – Reg Saunders makes waves on Bembridge beach and his wife teaches their young dog Pip old tricks in the 1950s. (MA)

The Saunders family rented this houseboat in Bembridge Harbour, 1953. The boat had no flush toilet and the elsan was emptied in the sea. (MA)

More Cowes than Bembridge, this cruiser next to theirs was nonetheless 'beached' in Bembridge Harbour in the 1950s.

Father and sons prepare a dinghy for a trip across the harbour in 1952. (MA)

A familiar sight off the island – a naval warship photographed from Bembridge beach, 1952.
(MA)

View from Gladys Bowe's Albion Hotel room, Freshwater 1988. Gladys retired to the island 'because of its peaceful air away from the rat race'. (GB)

Alum Chine suspension bridge and Cliff Drive, c1907. (JO)

UNION-CASTLE LINE INTERMEDIATE STEAMER "CARISBROOK CASTLE."     7,594 TONS.

Union Castle steamer *Carisbrooke Castle* brought troops back from the east: Martin Blane recalls 'Anchoring off the Isle of Wight, I remember thinking how green it all was'. (JO)

The lifeboat at Yarmouth c1978. Gladys Bowe remembers 'Sir Alec Rose launched the new lifeboat. Chale was dangerous and yachtsmen sometimes went out when it wasn't safe'. (GB)

Locomotive No 17 *Seaview* immaculate at Ryde Shed yard, 1 July 1953, and appropriately named, for an island where the sea is never far away. (BKBG)

Blackgang Chine 1975 – developed as scenic gardens in 1843. Set on the Chine's steeply wooded slopes and divided into theme areas, this is frontierland. (VFC)

Fantasyland, Blackgang Chine 1975. Which is the greatest horror; the mouth of hell or Cliff Church's fashionable flares? (VFC)

Sylvia Church and niece enjoy the continuous chair lift near the multi-coloured sands of Alum Bay, 1975. (VFC)

Visitors make sure they don't forget their postcards here on sale at Blackgang in the summer of 1975. (VFC)

The modern card – St Agnes Church, Freshwater Bay, inspired by a watercoloour design. The sometimes leaky 1908 thatched church was built on land given by Lord Tennyson. (NJC/LB)

New-port
You Cannot bottle.

Freshwater
You Cannot drink.

Cowes
You Cannot Milk.

Peculiar Properties
of the
Isle of Wight

Needles
You Cannot thread.

This postcard from long ago says much about the Isle of Wight and its 'peculiar properties'.
Wish you were here.